Acknowledgm

First of all, thank You, Jesus, for helping to get our words on paper and partnering us with the right people to get this project done. Your timing is always perfect, You are always good.

We greatly appreciate Patricia Bollmann for editing Firm Foundations and making us look good.

To our dear Ana Gleason, thank you for encouraging us, more than once, to publish Firm Foundations.

Thank you to Salvador Rodriguez, Judith Tartaglia, and Christina Cortez for translating Firm Foundations to Spanish.

To our precious church, First United Pentecostal Church of Fort Madison, thank you for all of your feedback and encouragement. We love you.

Finally, thank you to the UPCI District of Iowa for your love, support, and kind words. We are thankful to be a part of such a great district.

Contents

Week 1 - Introduction To The Bible   5-12

Week 2 - The Need For a Savior   13-16

Week 3 - How to be Saved   17-22

Week 4 - Seeking And Responding to God   23-28

Week 5 - Righteous Living   29-34

Week 6 - The Great Commission & Living in Power   35-40

Week 1 – Introduction to the Bible

Welcome to Firm Foundations! We are so glad you are here. We hope you enjoy each week's session as we lay a firm foundation using the building blocks of knowledge and truth

This first session is an introduction to the outline of the Word of God. We will discuss how the books of the Bible are categorized and why they are organized this way. We will explore fun facts about the Word of God and its history. We will discuss historical texts and archaeological discoveries that agree with the Word. If you have ever felt intimidated about studying the Bible, we hope this session will banish your worry and replace it with excitement for the Word of God and all the treasures within.

Point #1: The Bible was written over a period of about _____ years. Records of events, words of wisdom, letters, poems, songs, and so on were written by God's people as He worked in their lives and spoke into their hearts what He wanted to say to mankind. II Timothy 3:16 explains the *purpose* of the Word, saying, "All scripture is given by inspiration of God, and is profitable for doctrine, for reproof, for correction, for instruction in righteousness."

How did the sixty-six books that make up the Bible come together?
Up until the seventeenth century, different church bodies were trusting random books and letters that claimed to be God breathed. Many texts told exaggerated versions of events (like biased news stories we see in modern times), or they sent letters using someone else's name (like when your Facebook friend gets hacked, and their account sends you a sketchy link). So in 1604, King James commissioned a council of about fifty Bible and language scholars to evaluate all the ancient texts using a set of approved rules to determine which texts were genuine and accurate. The council ended up with the sixty-six books that, when combined, became the King James Bible of 1611.

The books of the Bible can be categorized based on who and what they focus on and what type of text they are. Knowing *about* each book of the Bible can help us understand what is written *in* each book. The books of the Bible can be broken down into nine major categories.

> ➤ First, we have the Old Testament and the New Testament: there are four categories in the Old Testament and five in the New Testament.

Old Testament
Genesis–Deuteronomy: _____
The books of the Law explain creation, God's original plan for man, and how mankind went wrong. These books show the Lord choosing a man named Abraham and his descendants (the Jewish people) —specifically Abraham's descendants through his grandson Jacob, also known as Israel (Genesis 32:28)—to be the people He used to bring mankind back to Him. These books also describe how God revealed His nature and expectations through the Law (more about this later) and how He revealed His love by remaining faithful to them in spite of their countless transgressions against Him. Genesis through Deuteronomy are important to understand because the rest of the books in the Bible refer back to promises God made, warnings He gave, and expectations He laid out.

Additional Scriptures

John 1:1

Ephesians 6:17

Joshua 1:8

Psalm 119:89

Hebrews 4:12

Psalm 1:2

II Timothy 2:15

Psalm 119:105

John 10:35

Deuteronomy 4:2

Revelation 22:18-19

II Peter 1:20-21

Side Note:

Moses wrote all five books of the Law: Genesis, Exodus, Leviticus, Numbers, and Deuteronomy.

Joshua–Esther: _____

These books follow the children (descendants) of Israel and what they experienced as a growing nation. We read about the political and spiritual choices this nation made, problems they faced, times that God intervened on their behalf, and situations where God allowed them to face the consequences of not living as He required.

- I & II Samuel and I & II Kings cover political history (wars, kings, rulers).

- I & II Chronicles cover religious history.

Job–Song of Solomon: _____

All the books of the Bible have a special way of speaking to us, but the wisdom literature or poetical books comprise a unique category in the way we can relate to them: this collection of wise sayings, experiences, and practical advice meets us where we are. They speak to the things we have been through or are going through to give encouragement and direction in the times we may not know where to turn. Possibly considered as literature of "Lived Theology," we see how people lived, reacted, and advised as they tried to understand their relationship with God while going through real-life situations. Many chapters in these books contain great examples of how to praise, worship, give thanks, and pray to God.

Isaiah–Malachi: _____

People are imperfect, so it is not surprising that there were years—even decades—during which God's people were unfaithful to Him because of ignorance of the Law or because of their willful breaking of the Law. Books in the "Prophets" category detail the experiences of prophets God sent to correct the children of Israel when the people were living lives that hurt and angered Him.

New Testament

Matthew–John: _____

Jesus' death on the cross gave mankind a true chance at redemption. While Jesus was on Earth, He interacted with us and was an example for us. What Jesus did for us and the lessons He taught were so important that they had to be recorded. The Gospels are four different perspectives of His life, death, and resurrection: the perspectives of Matthew, Mark, Luke, and John. For example, in Mark and Luke, the same storm is described in slightly different ways because of what the writer and audiences would tend to focus on. Reading each of these books is important in getting a full picture of who Jesus is and what He did. Each writer highlights different actions and different attributes of Christ because their focus when writing was to reach different groups of people.

Side Note:

The Four Gospels and Their Primary Audiences

Matthew: The Jews

Mark: The Romans

Luke: The Greeks

John: Everyone

Side Note:

When you see red text in the Bible, those are the words of Jesus.

Side Note:

Reading the four Gospels is one of the best ways to get to know Jesus and His character. Also, through reading about how He lived and communicated with people, we have a perfect example of how we should be communicating with others and living our lives.

Acts: _____

This book is called "Acts" because it describes the *acts* of the apostles after Jesus ascended into Heaven. Acts is the beginning of the New Testament church, of which we are a part. In the Book of Acts, we see the establishment of the apostles' doctrine, which is the truth we know, teach, and live by. We see Jesus inviting all people to become His children—not just the Jews. Because the early church in Acts was taught and led by people who learned directly *from* Jesus, we can use the events in this book as examples of what we should still be doing as a modern church today. God's plan of salvation has not changed.

➤ Ephesians 2:20 says, "And are built upon the foundation of the apostles and prophets, Jesus Christ himself being the chief corner stone."

➤ Galatians 3:28 says, "There is neither Jew nor Greek, there is neither bond nor free, there is neither male nor female: for ye are all one in Christ Jesus."

Romans–Philemon: _____

These are letters written by Paul to established churches, groups of people who had already experienced salvation according to the Book of Acts (baptism in Jesus' name and the gift of the Holy Ghost). These books do not describe how to *be* saved; they describe how to *remain* saved and live properly as children of God. Paul was aware of specific struggles each church was having, so he wrote to them with instructions for correcting these issues. The same problems that existed in churches of that time still exist in churches of our time, so these letters are equally relevant to us. These letters were also meant to encourage the churches. Again, the purpose of the Word of God is stated in II Timothy 3:16, saying, "All scripture is given by inspiration of God, and is profitable for doctrine, for reproof, for correction, for instruction in righteousness."

Hebrews–Jude: _____

These books or letters have their own category because they were not written by Paul. However, they are similar and agree with Paul's letters in that they were written to established saints and established churches—not to people who needed to be taught how to be saved. Just like Paul's letters, these letters target issues in modern churches and should be taken as instruction and correction.

> **SIDE NOTE:**
> James and Jude were Jesus' half-brothers.

Revelation: _____

The Lord revealed the future of the world to John through a vision. That vision is described in the Book of Revelation so that future generations would know what to expect. We read about the wonderful things promised to the children of God and the terrifying end promised to God's enemies. John describes what the world will be like right before Jesus returns; as a result, we can look for what he described, and those are signs that Jesus is coming soon.

> **SIDE NOTE:**
> Old Testament books can help you understand Jewish customs, and that understanding brings clarity to references in this prophetic book.

➤ Other prophecy-heavy passages are Matthew 24 and II Timothy 3.

> **SIDE NOTE:**
>
> **Groups of letters were named based on the church or person to whom they were written.** For example, "Romans" is the name for Paul's letters to the church of Rome; "Titus" is the name for Paul's letter to a minister named Titus; and "I Corinthians" and "II Corinthians" are the names for Paul's letters to the church at Corinth.

OLD TESTAMENT

The Law
- Genesis
- Exodus
- Leviticus
- Numbers
- Deuteronomy

History
- Joshua
- Judges
- Ruth
- I Samuel
- II Samuel
- I Kings
- II Kings
- I Chronicles
- II Chronicles
- Ezra
- Nehemiah
- Esther

Wisdom
- Job
- Psalms
- Proverbs
- Ecclesiastes
- Song of Solomon

Prophets
- Isaiah
- Jeremiah
- Lamentations
- Ezekiel
- Daniel
- Hosea
- Joel
- Amos
- Obadiah
- Jonah
- Micah
- Nahum
- Habakkuk
- Zephaniah
- Haggai
- Zechariah
- Malachi

NEW TESTAMENT

Gospels
- Matthew
- Mark
- Luke
- John

Church History
- Acts

Letters from Paul to Churches and Friends
- Romans
- I Corinthians
- II Corinthians
- Galatians
- Ephesians
- Philippians
- Colossians
- I Thessalonians
- II Thessalonians
- I Timothy
- II Timothy
- Titus
- Philemon

General Letters (From Other People)
- Hebrews
- James
- I Peter
- II Peter
- I John
- II John
- III John
- Jude

Prophecy
- Revelation

Point #2: The Bible is a collection of texts that records historical events, some of which are reported in more than one book. The books of the Bible are mostly in chronological order, but not completely so. To achieve a perfect chronological order of events, entire chapters would have to be moved elsewhere in the timeline.

Books that cover the same historical times (between King Saul and the Exile): I & II Samuel, I & II Kings, I & II Chronicles.

Point #3: Even though the books of the Bible were written over a timespan of 1500 years (in different locations and by _____ different authors), these sixty-six books do not contradict each other. It is helpful to know the books of the Bible agree with each other because that means they can be cross-referenced to provide clarity about certain topics. If you want to better understand what a verse or a passage means, there is another verse or passage elsewhere in the Bible that can help!

> - Proverbs 30:5 says, "Every word of God is pure: he is a shield unto them that put their trust in him."
>
> - II Timothy 3:16 says, "All scripture is given by inspiration of God, and is profitable for doctrine, for reproof, for correction, for instruction in righteousness."

> **SIDE NOTE:**
> The eras and cultures these authors lived in were so diverse that it would have been impossible for their sentiments to agree with each other and be entirely accurate—UNLESS they were directed by God. (See I Thessalonians 2:13.)

Many historical texts and archaeological finds agree with the Bible by describing or mentioning events and people that are recorded in the Bible. Here are three quick examples:

Josephus (jo-SEE-fuss)

Josephus was a man born in Jerusalem about four years after Jesus was crucified. Author Josh McDowell, in *The New Evidence That Demands a Verdict,* cites professor John P. Meier's statement that Josephus "was by turns a Jewish aristocrat, a priestly politician, a not-so-eager commander of rebel troops in Galilee during the First Jewish Revolt against Rome, a tricky turncoat, a Jewish historian in the pay of the Flavian emperors, and a supposed Pharisee" who "served the Romans as mediator and interpreter during the rest of the revolt." So it is interesting to find that Josephus wrote the following:

> *Now there was about this time Jesus, a wise man . . . for he was a doer of wonderful works, a teacher of such men as receive the truth with pleasure. He drew over to him both many of the Jews, and many of the Gentiles . . . And when Pilate, at the suggestion of the principal men among us, had condemned him to the cross, those that loved him at the first did not forsake him . . . And the tribe of Christians so named from him are not extinct at this day.*

Additionally, before Jesus was born, the Jewish people had what we call the Old Testament, but they called it the Tanakh. The writings of Josephus are generally accepted by historians as accurate, and his writings mention the existence of the Tanakh within the Jewish community of the time. He even mentioned the three main categories into which the Jews separated the Tanakh: Torah, Prophets, and Writings.

Bishop Melito
Bishop Melito was the Bishop of Sardis in Turkey. In about A.D. 170, he wrote a letter to his friend that included the first known list of Old Testament books. This letter proves that we still have the same books they had over 1,800 years ago.

Walls of Jericho
The Bible describes the location of the city of Jericho with enough detail that an archaeologist, who originally wanted to *disprove* the Bible, decided to dig there. When they dug in that specific location, they discovered not only the city but also the sunken walls!

Excavations of John Garstang at Jericho showing the remains of the city destroyed by the Israelites in about 1400 B.C.

Exterior of the retaining wall in Kenyon's west trench.

Aerial view of Jericho, looking south. The trenches and squares visible today are from Kathleen Kenyon's excavations in the 1950s and the more recent Italian-Palestinian excavation which began in 1997.

*Bishop Melito reference from Josh McDowell's book *The New Evidence That Demands a Verdict*

*Walls of Jerico Pictures from *https://christianpublishinghouse.co/2017/06/02/the-walls-of-jericho/*

MY NOTES

Week 2 – The Need for a Savior

In this session we will discuss our need for a Savior. We will explore how sin came into the world, what sin is, and why we need to be saved from a sinful life. We will also discuss how Jesus Christ redeemed us and became our Savior. Sin is often a taboo subject and has become a "trigger word" in our society. Yet sin is real, and we must become aware of it in our life. The goal of this session is to bring understanding and godly conviction, which are essential in a walk with the Lord.

> ➤ James 4:17 says, " Therefore to him that knoweth to do good, and doeth it not, to him it is sin."
>
> ➤ Romans 3:23 says, "For all have sinned, and come short of the glory of God."

Side Note:
"Sin" was an old archery term. "A sin" was the same thing as "a miss." We can "miss" out with God when we disobey Him.

Additional Scriptures

I John 4:8
James 4:17
Romans 3:23
John 3:16-18
Acts 2:40
Matthew 26:28
Leviticus 17:11
II Peter 3:9
Deuteronomy 6:4
Acts 4:12
Isaiah 9:6
Acts 9:5
John 10:30
I Timothy 3:16
John 14:6-9
John 20:26-29

Point #1: God created mankind to love and be loved by Him. When you love someone, you choose them over other people or priorities. Jesus chose not to make us like robotic servants who were programmed to compliment Him all the time. Those expressions would not have been motivated by real love. Instead, Jesus gave us the power of choice—the ability (free will) to choose Him or to reject Him. God was completely alone before He created the heavens and the earth. And although He is God, He felt the same desire we feel to have someone to love us. But because there was no one beside Him, He had to CREATE human beings and hope they would choose to love Him.

> ➤ _____: If God and Jesus were separate "persons" existing together before time began, why would God want or need children? Why create people to be His children if He already had a pre-existent son? For such a desire to arise in God, Jesus would have to have been an insufficient son, which we know is not possible. The truth is there was no pre-existent Son. When the fullness of time came, God manifested Himself in flesh, and that manifestation was called the Son. (See Luke 1:31–33.)
>
> ➤ Deuteronomy 6:5 says, "And thou shalt love the LORD thy God with all thine heart, and with all thy soul, and with all thy might."

Point #2: Adam and Eve, the first humans God made, were created in innocence. They lived in a paradise called the Garden of Eden where everything they could possibly want or need was available to them. Being innocent, they did not have the ability to discern good from evil. They did, however, have the power of choice; they could choose to obey or disobey the Lord's command. Their choice to love and obey God or reject and disobey God came to bear when God told them not to eat from the Tree of the Knowledge of _____. Eating the fruit of that particular tree would mean death for them. Unfortunately, they chose to disobey God's command and were therefore exiled out of Paradise, and sin was introduced into the world.

The Tree of Knowledge of Good and Evil was not guarded or hidden; it was in the "midst of the garden." Only God's commandment stood between Adam and Eve and the tree.

> ➢ Genesis 2:17 says, "But of the tree of the knowledge of good and evil, thou shalt not eat of it: for in the day that thou eatest thereof thou shalt surely die."

> ➢ Joshua 24:15 says, "Choose you this day whom ye will serve."

Point #3: One of the creatures in the Garden was a serpent (the devil) who deceived Eve by slyly manipulating God's words. Adam and Eve allowed themselves to be persuaded by the serpent's deception, thus choosing to remove themselves from God's original plans in favor of a desire for "knowledge" and some temporary satisfaction.

> ➢ We are not to add or take away from the Word of God. If we do not know and understand what God's Word says, it is easy for us to be manipulated or deceived. If at any time we believe the Word of God is contradicting itself, we have simply misunderstood or "twisted" the Word. When we do this, it is to our own destruction. Revelation 22:18–19 says, "For I testify unto every man that heareth the words of the prophecy of this book, If any man shall add unto these things, God shall add unto him the plagues that are written in this book: and if any man shall take away from the words of the book of this prophecy, God shall take away his part out of the book of life, and out of the holy city, and from the things which are written in this book."

> ➢ _____ says, "As our beloved brother Paul also wrote to you according to the wisdom given him, as he does in all his letters when he speaks in them of these matters. There are some things in them that are hard to understand, which the ignorant and unstable twist to their own destruction." The Word does not contradict itself. Confusion arises when we try to reconcile a verse we understand with a verse we do not understand. This can be avoided only by studying the Word and discovering all the verses that pertain to a particular subject.

Point #4: Because Adam and Eve chose to eat of the forbidden tree, all peoples born thereafter are automatically born into iniquity (which means sin) and are in need of justification and redemption. Psalm 51:4–5 says, "Against thee, thee only, have I sinned, and done this evil in thy sight: that thou mightest be justified when thou speakest, and be clear when thou judgest. Behold, I was shapen in iniquity; and in sin did my mother conceive me." Our God is a _____ God, and justice demands payment for guilt. God could not go against His nature and accept mankind's guilt as if it were innocence. As God told Adam and Eve in His first warning, eating of the tree would mean death. They committed the crime and now would have to pay the price. Death is the loss of life; Adam and Eve lost their chance at living life in perfect communion with God.

> ➢ A Couple Examples That Might Help Us Understand the Relationship Shift after Sin
>
>   o Because light dispels darkness, and God is light, He therefore has to back away from us when we choose darkness.
>
>   o Your spouse cheating on you would cause a rift between you two, so it makes sense that God would back away from Adam and Eve when they chose to "cheat" on Him.

> ➢ Thankfully, after mankind sinned, God's judgment and love came together, providing mercy.

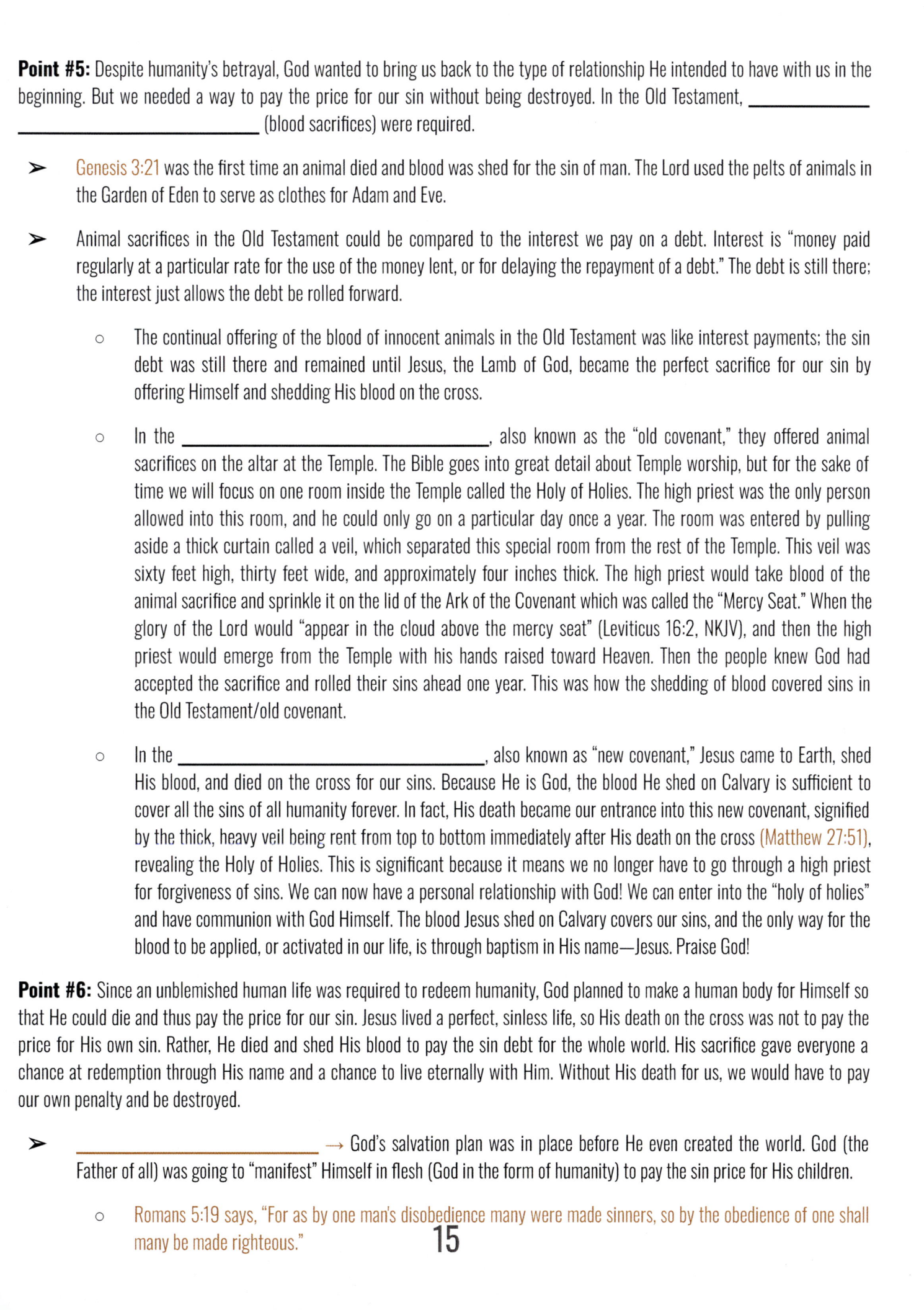

Point #5: Despite humanity's betrayal, God wanted to bring us back to the type of relationship He intended to have with us in the beginning. But we needed a way to pay the price for our sin without being destroyed. In the Old Testament, _____ _____ (blood sacrifices) were required.

➤ Genesis 3:21 was the first time an animal died and blood was shed for the sin of man. The Lord used the pelts of animals in the Garden of Eden to serve as clothes for Adam and Eve.

➤ Animal sacrifices in the Old Testament could be compared to the interest we pay on a debt. Interest is "money paid regularly at a particular rate for the use of the money lent, or for delaying the repayment of a debt." The debt is still there; the interest just allows the debt be rolled forward.

   o The continual offering of the blood of innocent animals in the Old Testament was like interest payments; the sin debt was still there and remained until Jesus, the Lamb of God, became the perfect sacrifice for our sin by offering Himself and shedding His blood on the cross.

   o In the _____, also known as the "old covenant," they offered animal sacrifices on the altar at the Temple. The Bible goes into great detail about Temple worship, but for the sake of time we will focus on one room inside the Temple called the Holy of Holies. The high priest was the only person allowed into this room, and he could only go on a particular day once a year. The room was entered by pulling aside a thick curtain called a veil, which separated this special room from the rest of the Temple. This veil was sixty feet high, thirty feet wide, and approximately four inches thick. The high priest would take blood of the animal sacrifice and sprinkle it on the lid of the Ark of the Covenant which was called the "Mercy Seat." When the glory of the Lord would "appear in the cloud above the mercy seat" (Leviticus 16:2, NKJV), and then the high priest would emerge from the Temple with his hands raised toward Heaven. Then the people knew God had accepted the sacrifice and rolled their sins ahead one year. This was how the shedding of blood covered sins in the Old Testament/old covenant.

   o In the _____, also known as "new covenant," Jesus came to Earth, shed His blood, and died on the cross for our sins. Because He is God, the blood He shed on Calvary is sufficient to cover all the sins of all humanity forever. In fact, His death became our entrance into this new covenant, signified by the thick, heavy veil being rent from top to bottom immediately after His death on the cross (Matthew 27:51), revealing the Holy of Holies. This is significant because it means we no longer have to go through a high priest for forgiveness of sins. We can now have a personal relationship with God! We can enter into the "holy of holies" and have communion with God Himself. The blood Jesus shed on Calvary covers our sins, and the only way for the blood to be applied, or activated in our life, is through baptism in His name—Jesus. Praise God!

Point #6: Since an unblemished human life was required to redeem humanity, God planned to make a human body for Himself so that He could die and thus pay the price for our sin. Jesus lived a perfect, sinless life, so His death on the cross was not to pay the price for His own sin. Rather, He died and shed His blood to pay the sin debt for the whole world. His sacrifice gave everyone a chance at redemption through His name and a chance to live eternally with Him. Without His death for us, we would have to pay our own penalty and be destroyed.

➤ _____ → God's salvation plan was in place before He even created the world. God (the Father of all) was going to "manifest" Himself in flesh (God in the form of humanity) to pay the sin price for His children.

   o Romans 5:19 says, "For as by one man's disobedience many were made sinners, so by the obedience of one shall many be made righteous."

MY NOTES

Week 3 – How to Be Saved

This session builds off of last week's "The Need for a Savior." We will review what sin is and then learn how to be saved through repentance, being baptized in Jesus' name, and being filled with His Spirit. We will discuss the oneness of God through biblical evidence. I hope you leave this session filled with understanding, hope, and joy because of your bright future through salvation.

_____ means missing the mark; walking away from God's plan. James 4:17 says, "Therefore to him that knoweth to do good, and doeth it not, to him it is sin."

_____ means to turn about (like today's military term "about face"—180 degrees or the opposite direction). Repentance is turning away from sin and moving toward God and how He wants you to live (the mark).

Point #1: Repentance
The first step is _____. This type of repentance comes from a desire to change your life. You recognize that the life you are living is not good enough; you have been living according to the dictates of your sinful nature. You know you need to change. True repentance on this level will include forgiveness (of others and self) and restitution. *Forgiveness* is giving all the past hurts, grudges, and failures to God. *Restitution* means righting the wrongs you have committed.

Why: Matthew 6:14–15 (NIV) says, "For if you forgive other people when they sin against you, your heavenly Father will also forgive you. But if you do not forgive others their sins, your Father will not forgive your sins."

_____ is an integral part of salvation. If you want to receive forgiveness, you must forgive.
- ➤ Jesus' death on the cross paid the price of sin for all, including those who have hurt you.

- ➤ God made the rules, and if we break those rules, we have sinned. Jesus decides who will enter Heaven. By thinking we are justified to withhold forgiveness, we are suggesting that we know better or have more authority than God. We do not decide who deserves forgiveness; we bestow on Earth the forgiveness that God already offers in Heaven. That is our obligation. Doing anything less than—or contrary to—that is an insult to the God we claim to represent and serve.

_____ is the "dirty work" of cleaning up our thoughts and behaviors. The key to success is allowing Jesus to help us turn away (repent) from one thing at a time. It is a journey of continual growth and change no matter where we are in our relationship with Him.
- ➤ Joshua 24:15 says, "Choose you this day whom ye will serve." Each day is a choice.

- ➤ A few great examples of repentance and forgiveness to study at home are II Corinthians 7:1, Matthew 18:21–35, and Psalm 51.

Additional Scriptures

John 16:7

John 14:26

Luke 24:49

Acts 1:4–5, 8

Mark 16:16–17

Mark 2:5–7

Acts 16:30–33

Acts 22:16

I Corinthians 14:18

Colossians 2:12

Deuteronomy 6:4

Isaiah 9:6

Isaiah 45:5

Point #2: Baptism

Baptism was not introduced as a new thing in the New Testament. It was a common Jewish ritual that signified spiritual cleansing and covenant. In the process of salvation, we must be baptized in Jesus' name. Acts 4:12 says, "Neither is there salvation in any other: for there is none other name under heaven given among men, whereby we must be saved." No other name can save anyone. By being baptized in Jesus' name, we are making a commitment/covenant to live for Him. This covenant brings us under the sacrifice that Jesus made on the cross, paying for all of our sin. Much like a marriage, we get God's name applied to our lives. We are also saying that we want a lifelong relationship with God and that we want to live in a way that is pleasing to Him.

Biblical baptism is properly done by full _____. The word "baptism" comes from the Greek verb "baptizo" meaning "to immerse" or "to submerge." Originally found in the ancient textile industries, the verb "baptizo" was applied to the process in which fabrics were dyed another color by submerging them in a pot or vat of pigment. Likewise, when we are wanting a change in our lives, we are completely submerged to symbolically bury the old man and apply the blood of Jesus to our lives. Just like a submerged garment, we should come out of the water with a new look and new values, letting God take every part of us and change it as He sees fit. Matthew 3:16 says that Jesus, at His baptism, came "up straightway out of the water" as our example.

> ➤ The apostle Peter compared the act of baptism to the Flood that covered the whole Earth: "Which sometime were disobedient, when once the longsuffering of God waited in the days of Noah, while the ark was a preparing, wherein few, that is, eight souls were saved by water. The like figure whereunto even baptism doth also now save us (not the putting away of the filth of the flesh, but the answer of a good conscience toward God,) by the resurrection of Jesus Christ" (I Peter 3:20–21).

> ➤ Biblical baptism is also compared to being buried. Burying someone means covering them completely with dirt, just as we should be completely covered by the waters of baptism. Colossians 2:12 says, "Buried with him in baptism, wherein also ye are risen with him through the faith of the operation of God, who hath raised him from the dead."

Point #3: Holy Ghost

Holy Ghost or Holy Spirit are interchangeable terms that mean the same thing. It is vital to know that receiving the Holy Ghost, which is God's Spirit, is a gift and promise of God that is available to all (Acts 2:39). Just as a birthday gift or Christmas present is wrapped, the Holy Ghost is not truly received until you have opened the gift. "Speaking in tongues" is the _____ that you have received the Holy Ghost. Acts 2:4 says, "They were all filled with the Holy Ghost, and began to speak with other tongues, as the Spirit gave them utterance [command/voice]." Jesus foretold of this promise that was to come in John 7:37–39: "In the last day, that great day of the feast, Jesus stood and cried, saying, If any man thirst, let him come unto me, and drink. He that believeth on me, as the scripture hath said, out of his belly shall flow rivers of living water. (But this spake he of the Spirit, which they that believe on Him should receive: for the Holy Ghost was not yet given; because that Jesus was not yet glorified.)"

Additional Scriptures

John 1:1, 14

John 10:30

John 14:6, 9

Acts 9:4–5

Acts 6:5–6

1 Timothy 4:14

Ephesians 4:5

1 John 2:1

Revelation 7:10, 17

Revelation 21:5

God was purposeful in making our mouths a part of the evidence of us having received the Holy Ghost. James 3:8 says, "But the tongue can no man tame." Therefore, the submitting of our _____ to the Spirit of God is what can bring us to this precious promise of receiving the Holy Ghost. We cannot calculate, manipulate or imitate this; it is God given. We must simply believe and be available to receive. It is truly amazing how God has enabled all people to receive and experience this promise. Genesis 11 opens by saying everyone on earth spoke the same language, but as they were building the Tower of Babel, God changed their languages. In the New Testament, the Lord again chose the tongue to reveal His power. We have biblical examples of people speaking in tongues before baptism without hands being laid on them (Acts 10:44–48) and after baptism with the laying on of hands (Acts 8:12–17; 19:6). However, the first step is positioning yourself to hear and respond to the Word of God. Repentance is an incredible step, as it is our response to hearing the Word of God (Acts 2:37). Receiving the Holy Ghost can happen anywhere, anytime.

> **SIDE NOTE:**
> You may experience or see people "lay hands" on one another in church. The apostles laid hands on new believers and old believers. The New Testament also associates the laying on of hands with the giving of authority or designation of a person to a position of responsibility (Acts 6:5–6; 13:3; I Timothy 4:14).

Receiving the Holy Ghost can sound different depending on the person. Some people begin by speaking clearly in tongues, while others may have stammering lips or stuttering words before speaking fluently in the language the Lord gives them. It can certainly seem different or extraordinary to speak words that are not of our native tongue. But understand that this is absolutely and unapologetically a God-given promise that is an essential component of receiving and experiencing His plan of salvation. Paul, who wrote many books in the New Testament, spoke of this experience and thanked Jesus for it. He said in I Corinthians 14:18, "I thank my God, I speak with tongues more than ye all." Besides being the initial sign that we have received the Holy Ghost, speaking in tongues also helps us pray more effectively (Romans 8:26). Speaking in tongues is a sign that you are a believer (Mark 16:17). Rest assured, if you are actively hearing the Word of God, repenting, seeking, and believing, the Holy Ghost will become evident in your life and you will speak in tongues! Just as repentance and baptism in Jesus' name are essential for salvation, so is receiving the Holy Ghost.

Point #4: Oneness of God

Since our salvation is all about our relationship with God, our Savior, it is essential that we understand His true nature. He is not a Trinity, meaning "one God in three persons, the state of being three, a group of three people." People who believe in a triune God are called "Trinitarians," and they typically baptize "in the name of the Father, and of the Son, and of the Holy Ghost" (Matthew 28:19). In reality, the word "trinity" is not found anywhere in the Bible. Furthermore, the apostles rightly interpreted the name of the Father, and of the Son, and of the Holy Ghost as Jesus. (See the Book of Acts references on page 13 in the side note.)

God is _____, not three in one, an absolute fact emphasized throughout the Bible. Genesis 1:1 says, "In the beginning God created the heaven and the earth." It was God who created, not gods. God's word is clear—He is One. All three titles refer to the same "One": God (Colossians 2:9; I John 5:7). There is one God, and He is Lord. He has revealed Himself to humanity as the Father (Creator), the Son (Savior), and the Holy Ghost (indwelling Spirit). Jesus is the name of our God and Lord. Just as you may have certain titles (you are a father, son, daughter, niece, friend, employee, retiree), you have a name. We refer to ourselves as Oneness because we believe in one God. We, as Oneness believers, invoke the name of Jesus—who is the Father, the Son, and the Holy Ghost—when administering baptism. John wrote about his vision, "And immediately I was in the spirit, and, behold, a throne was set in heaven, and one sat on the throne" (Revelation 4:2). How glorious that we serve one God who has granted us the knowledge to know His name—Jesus! Hebrews 4:16 tells us to "come boldly unto the throne of grace," and we know the One who sits on that throne! The chart on the next page will further inform your personal study.

Wheel of Prophecy
Who Is GOD?

God Is a Spirit
John 4:23-24
Acts 7:48-49
Acts 17:24-28
Psalm 139:7-12
I Kings 8:27
Jeremiah 23:23-24

There Is but One God
Deuteronomy 6:4-9
Mark 12:28-32
Malachi 2:10
Isaiah 44:6-8
Isaiah 45:2-6, 21-23
Isaiah 46:8-9
I Corinthians 8:4-6
Ephesians 4:5-6
I Timothy 2:5
James 2:19
Revelation 4:2-3

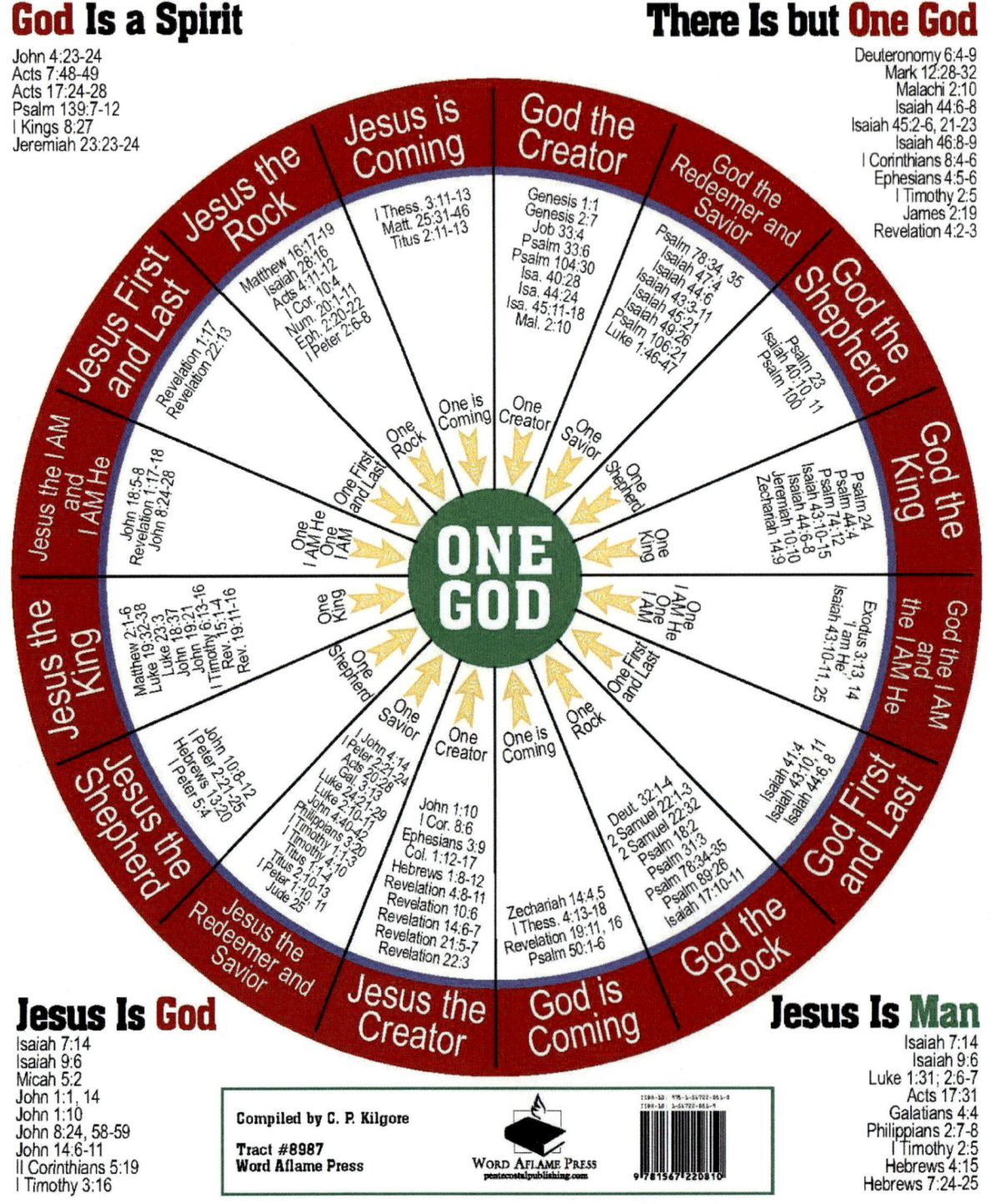

Jesus Is God
Isaiah 7:14
Isaiah 9:6
Micah 5:2
John 1:1, 14
John 1:10
John 8:24, 58-59
John 14:6-11
II Corinthians 5:19
I Timothy 3:16

Compiled by C. P. Kilgore
Tract #8987
Word Aflame Press

Jesus Is Man
Isaiah 7:14
Isaiah 9:6
Luke 1:31; 2:6-7
Acts 17:31
Galatians 4:4
Philippians 2:7-8
I Timothy 2:5
Hebrews 4:15
Hebrews 7:24-25

© Pentecostal Resources Group. Used by permission. All rights reserved.

MY NOTES

Week 4 – Seeking and Responding to God

This week we will discuss praise, worship, prayer, the voice of God, and free will. It is important to know what each of these terms means and why it is significant. I hope by the end of this session you will feel excited and equipped to take your relationship with Jesus to the next level.

Point #1:
- _____
  (VERB/ACTION) to express warm approval or admiration of
  (NOUN/THING) the expression of approval or admiration for someone or something

- _____
  (NOUN/THING) the feeling or expression of reverence and adoration for a deity
  (VERB/ACTION) to show reverence and adoration for (a deity); honor with religious rites.
  *The "wor-" in "worship" stems from the "wor-" in "worth." Worship is a reverent acknowledgment of God's worth—how powerful and perfect He is.

Praise and worship are similar but not the same. Praise is an enthusiastic display of thankfulness or admiration. Worship is a humble display of awe for who God is.

In our daily lives, we praise people all the time. We tell our friends they did a great job. We clap after a song at a band concert. We go to football games and shout, clap, jump, and cheer when our team scores. These excited expressions of approval and appreciation for other people's accomplishments are examples of praise.

When praise is directed toward God in church, that praise should surpass the excitement and noisiness of our praise for other people. When someone says, "Praise the Lord," they are inviting us to express our excitement and appreciation for the things Jesus has done. We applaud at the end of worship songs for Jesus, not for the worship team. God's deeds deserve some noise!

Acts and words of worship are typically quieter; they are inspired by awe and respect for God. Picture the national anthem before a football game. To show their respect, people will stand, take off their hats, be quiet, and place their hand over their heart while facing the flag.

When we worship God, we do so because we recognize how perfect and powerful He is compared to our imperfect and powerless selves. We are showing that we recognize and submit to His authority. When worshiping in the church setting, we show reverence, and we feel and experience awe for God. Bowing our heads, kneeling, crying, feeling the overwhelming presence of God—that is worship. It is a humble response to the recognition of who He is and what He has done.

Though praise and worship must be part of our church services, you do not need to be in the church building to worship and praise. You can and should praise and worship Jesus even when you are alone. When you are at home doing chores, you can put on some worship music and start worshiping and praising God. You can also worship and praise in your "prayer closet." Just as a husband and wife should express their appreciation for each other continually, you should be showing God your excitement and awe for Him more than once or twice a week.

Additional Scriptures

Psalm 150
Psalm 98:4
Ezra 3:11
Acts 3:8
Exodus 34:14
Genesis 24:26
Matthew 2:11
Job 1:20
Psalm 95:6
John 4:24
Psalm 145:2
I Samuel 1:3
Matthew 6:7
I Timothy 2:1
Psalm 77:1
Isaiah 38:5
Acts 10:1-4

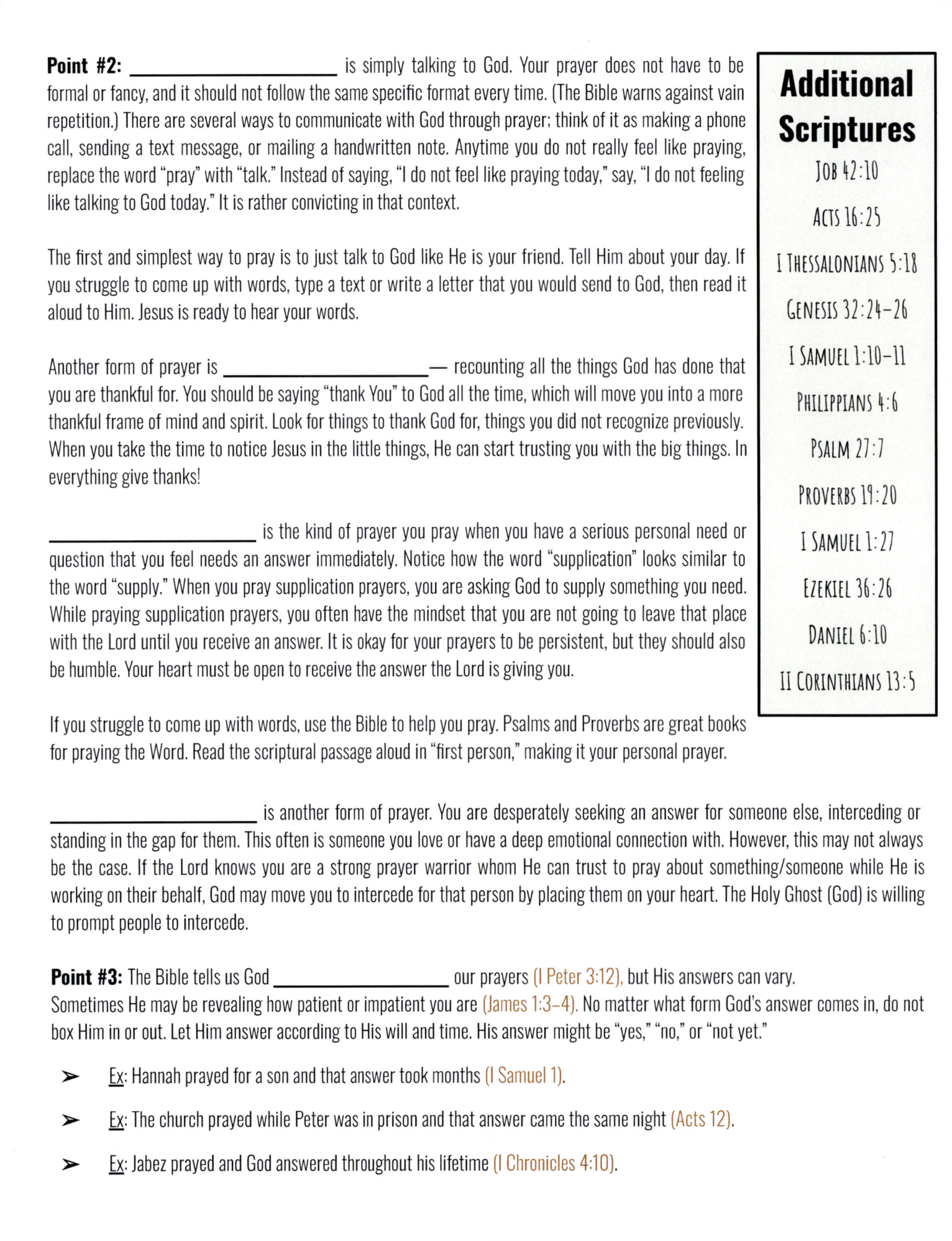

Point #2: _____ is simply talking to God. Your prayer does not have to be formal or fancy, and it should not follow the same specific format every time. (The Bible warns against vain repetition.) There are several ways to communicate with God through prayer; think of it as making a phone call, sending a text message, or mailing a handwritten note. Anytime you do not really feel like praying, replace the word "pray" with "talk." Instead of saying, "I do not feel like praying today," say, "I do not feeling like talking to God today." It is rather convicting in that context.

The first and simplest way to pray is to just talk to God like He is your friend. Tell Him about your day. If you struggle to come up with words, type a text or write a letter that you would send to God, then read it aloud to Him. Jesus is ready to hear your words.

Another form of prayer is _____— recounting all the things God has done that you are thankful for. You should be saying "thank You" to God all the time, which will move you into a more thankful frame of mind and spirit. Look for things to thank God for, things you did not recognize previously. When you take the time to notice Jesus in the little things, He can start trusting you with the big things. In everything give thanks!

_____ is the kind of prayer you pray when you have a serious personal need or question that you feel needs an answer immediately. Notice how the word "supplication" looks similar to the word "supply." When you pray supplication prayers, you are asking God to supply something you need. While praying supplication prayers, you often have the mindset that you are not going to leave that place with the Lord until you receive an answer. It is okay for your prayers to be persistent, but they should also be humble. Your heart must be open to receive the answer the Lord is giving you.

If you struggle to come up with words, use the Bible to help you pray. Psalms and Proverbs are great books for praying the Word. Read the scriptural passage aloud in "first person," making it your personal prayer.

_____ is another form of prayer. You are desperately seeking an answer for someone else, interceding or standing in the gap for them. This often is someone you love or have a deep emotional connection with. However, this may not always be the case. If the Lord knows you are a strong prayer warrior whom He can trust to pray about something/someone while He is working on their behalf, God may move you to intercede for that person by placing them on your heart. The Holy Ghost (God) is willing to prompt people to intercede.

Point #3: The Bible tells us God _____ our prayers (I Peter 3:12), but His answers can vary. Sometimes He may be revealing how patient or impatient you are (James 1:3–4). No matter what form God's answer comes in, do not box Him in or out. Let Him answer according to His will and time. His answer might be "yes," "no," or "not yet."

➤ Ex: Hannah prayed for a son and that answer took months (I Samuel 1).

➤ Ex: The church prayed while Peter was in prison and that answer came the same night (Acts 12).

➤ Ex: Jabez prayed and God answered throughout his lifetime (I Chronicles 4:10).

Additional Scriptures

Job 42:10

Acts 16:25

I Thessalonians 5:18

Genesis 32:24–26

I Samuel 1:10–11

Philippians 4:6

Psalm 27:7

Proverbs 19:20

I Samuel 1:27

Ezekiel 36:26

Daniel 6:10

II Corinthians 13:5

Point #4: Just as God wants to hear from us, He wants to be heard by us (Revelation 2:11). Therefore, we need to _____ for His voice. But how can we tell when it is God talking and not our flesh or the enemy?

When God speaks to us, it will ALWAYS line up with His Word. Jesus would never give you an answer that would contradict His Word.

➤ Ex: God would never tell you to "get even" with someone. His Word says vengeance belongs to Him (Deuteronomy 32:35). Therefore, if you feel a need to get even with someone, you know that thought was not from the Lord.

Many times, the voice of God can be like a still small voice (I Kings 19:11-12) or an impression in your heart or mind. Too often we dismiss these impressions as coincidences. If you obey what you believe God is directing you to do, it will reveal His voice, His presence, or the reward He has for you.

God will also use His Word, the Bible, to respond to questions or requests (II Corinthians 12:8-9), which is why it is so important to read the Word daily (Joshua 1:8). Reading the Bible opens your "spiritual ears" to His voice in your life. It helps you distinguish between His voice, your own voice, and the devil's voice.

➤ God can use His Word to give you an answer about why something is happening or how you are supposed to act in a certain situation. The Bible is full of instances in which He called people to do this or that. If He asked people to do something back then, He might ask you to do something similar.

➤ After you step out in obedience to what you think is His voice, He can use His Word to reassure you that you were right. For instance, you might obey the still small voice and later read in His Word exactly what you heard/did.

God also speaks to you through the _____ (Romans 10:14, 17), or through things you are reading or watching (Luke 21:25). God is literally speaking at all times. It is up to you to recognize His voice. Remember whenever you think the Lord is speaking to you, it ALWAYS agrees with His Word.

Point #5: The things we are discussing in this session will be greatly impacted by what is in your heart. You must seek God with a sincere desire to connect with Him, as the Bible says, with our "_____" (Jeremiah 29:13). It is not enough to go through the motions in an effort to convince others or ourselves that we are perfect saints. When Jesus says something to us through preaching or through a song, we need to give an honest response. We must worship with true humility and reverence. God is not fooled by or satisfied with what LOOKS right but actually is insincere.

It may be difficult, but you should examine whether there is anything hindering your connection to God (II Corinthians 13:5). What distractions are taking time away from your relationship with God? Too much entertainment often occupies our time as well as other unimportant activities (Luke 10:41-42). Other issues may hinder how you feel toward God, such as unforgiveness, pride (thinking we do not need help), or looking to the things of God as duty rather than desire (Psalm 100:2).

Luke 18:10-14 is a parable (or story) of two men who went to the Temple to pray: one was a Pharisee and the other a publican. The proud Pharisee boasted about his obedience to the Law, thinking he was better than other men. The publican bowed his head and humbly asked God to forgive his sins, seeking God with his whole heart. What actions do you need to take so you can truly seek God from your heart? It begins and ends with your focus on pleasing Jesus at all times. Do the things you know are pleasing to Him (for example, praying, reading His Word, forgiving others, or singing praises). You will never go wrong when obeying His Word. Like water to a seed, the right responses and the process of time will produce what is needed. There will be mountaintops and valleys, ebbs and flows, but He is God of all. Stay consistent. Jesus is with you (Matthew 28:20).

> **Side Note:** A Pharisee was a Jewish religious sect of leaders and businessmen of the synagogues. They were considered righteous at that time.

Point #6: God has given us _____. That being the case, we can choose to let God do what He wants to do in our lives. In Luke 22:42, Jesus prayed, "Nevertheless not my will but thine be done." How do we make ourselves useful to the kingdom of God? We do our very best to allow Him to shape and mold us continually (Jeremiah 18:3-6). If we do not make ourselves available and useful, we become a stumbling block to ourselves and others around us.

> **Side Note:** A Publican was a Jew who would conspire with the Roman Empire. Often times they were a tax collector.

➤ Let God change your attitude, help you forgive, remove pride, renew your mind, and so on.

➤ Know that your circle of family, friends, and acquaintances matters. Relationships may need to be adjusted or even abandoned if they are not spiritually healthy.

➤ Be ready for 'divine appointments' throughout your day. For example - be sure to have a church card on you at all times so you can invite someone to the sanctuary for a service. Having the card is an act of faith that says, "God, I trust that you will lead me to someone." If you do not carry a church card, you are revealing to God that you do not plan on meeting someone who needs to experience the love of Christ.

➤ Even small choices can hinder the will of God in your life. For example, staying up late at night to watch a movie, resulting in less sleep, can impact the next day. Poor planning or time management can leave you without time to do things for God. You are thus unprepared for opportunities God wants to present to you. Matthew 6:33 helps you to realign with the words, "Seek ye first the kingdom of God and his righteousness; and all these things will be added unto you." Give Jesus your life and time and watch Him redeem it.

MY NOTES

Week 5 – Righteous Living

In this session we will discuss the ins and outs of living for God. We will cover fellowship, biblical giving, being the Lord's ambassadors, and why these things are important to maintain a healthy, consistent Christian lifestyle. This session will help set you up for success and good godly growth.

Additional Scriptures

II Corinthians 11:24-27
Hebrews 3:7-10
I Peter 3:17
John 3:12
Acts 2:1
I John 4:12
Acts 20:35
Matthew 23:23

Point #1: _____

Life happens to everyone. Whether a person is living for God or not, struggles and trials will still come their way. So do not be discouraged when challenges occur in your life. Do not believe the lie that your relationship with Jesus is not real when you are going through something difficult. Matthew 5:45 says, "That ye may be the children of your Father which is in heaven: for He maketh His sun to rise on the evil and on the good, and sendeth rain on the just and on the unjust."

Even though we are made a new creature when we receive the salvation experience, we need to continue walking with God every day, being careful to keep our focus on that relationship and nurturing our spiritual nature (II Corinthians 5:17; I Peter 3:21). We still live in a world full of sin and temptations. We can still be vulnerable to the lust of the flesh, the lust of the eye, and/or the pride of life. If we are not careful, we can still fall prey to our own weaknesses of mind and body (I Corinthians 9:27; 15:31; Matthew 16:24).

Our suffering might be a result of a spiritual attack, religious persecution, a foolish decision on our part, or simply the troubles that come with being human. Spiritual attacks happen when the enemy wants to stop our spiritual progress. Religious persecution comes from people who feel convicted or somehow threatened by the presence of God that resides in us. That is why the Bible says we should be thankful when we experience persecution for His sake (Acts 5:41). Foolish decisions often have negative consequences, so we always need to analyze our circumstances to see if there was a wiser step we could have taken to avoid the same issues in the future. Some issues, though, are unavoidable. Minor inconveniences and major suffering (anything from car trouble to cancer) are unfortunate realities that come with living in an imperfect, temporal world populated by imperfect people using things that do not last forever. Regardless of what category our suffering falls into, the proper response is ALWAYS to seek God's peace and guidance and to appreciate the strength, compassion, and comfort He provides.

Point #2: _____

Galatians 5:17 says, "For the flesh lusteth against the Spirit, and the Spirit against the flesh: and these are contrary the one to the other: so that ye cannot do the things that ye would." Our fleshly nature is contrary to the Spirit of God. Therefore, if we want to maintain our relationship with God, we must learn how to deny our flesh. Choosing to walk after the flesh will cause us to lose out on the blessings that come to us when the wonderful fruit of the Spirit is being produced in our lives (Galatians 5:17–23).

> ➤ Matthew 6:24 says, "No man can serve two masters: for either he will hate the one, and love the other; or else he will hold to the one, and despise the other. Ye cannot serve God and mammon [money]."

The natural world parallels the spiritual world. Psalm 119:105 says, "Thy word is a lamp unto my feet, and a light unto my path." The things we do in one world will affect the other world. For example, we cannot have a healthy spiritual life if we are doing things that are against the Word of God. Although doing good things will not on its own make for a good spiritual life, we can help our spiritual growth by replacing carnally driven things with spiritually driven things.

Point #3: _____

If Adam and Eve messed up in a perfect environment, we inevitably will mess up in this imperfect environment. How can we avoid sin? First, the definition of sin is "to miss the mark." Anything outside of the will of God is sin, thus the first part of avoiding sin is to know what God wants us to do (Genesis 4:7). In order to know this, we need to have a habit of Bible reading and prayer. What does His Word tell us to do? What does His Spirit tell us to do? Jesus gave us a fourfold personal ministry: "But I say unto you, Love your enemies, bless them that curse you, do good to them that hate you, and pray for them which despitefully use you, and persecute you" (Matthew 5:44).

Second, the earlier we respond to our sin, the easier it will be to repent; therefore, we should repent of the mistake as quickly as possible (Luke 5:8). Repentance is to turn *away* from the sin and *back* to what God wants us to do.

- Dealing with sins of omission (things we did not know were wrong at the time) will get easier once we realize they are there, as long as we are striving to live for God.

- Intentional sins (the working of iniquity) may be more difficult to truly repent of (Hebrews 10:26). We need to seek God's direction and conviction and let Him change our heart and will about the matter. Luke 22:42 says, "Father, if thou be willing, remove this cup from me: nevertheless not my will, but thine, be done."

Even small things need to be repented of because they can add up if we do not resolve them quickly through repentance. That is why daily "dying out" (repenting) is a necessary part of living a righteous life.

- Matthew 16:24 says, "Then said Jesus unto his disciples, If any man will come after me, let him deny himself, and take up his cross, and follow me."

Point #4: _____

Ecclesiastes 4:10 says, "For if they fall, the one will lift up his fellow: but woe to him that is alone when he falleth; for he hath not another to help him up." It is important that we spend time together so we can encourage each other, give feedback, and add joy to each other's lives. The church is the people, not the building. Scripture refers to us as the body of Christ. God does not want us isolated. We are meant to be one unit, a family. It is very difficult to be united and caring for each other if we never spend time together. If we find ourselves misunderstanding one another or having hard feelings toward each other, we probably need more fellowship.

- Acts 2:42 says, "And they continued steadfastly in the apostles' doctrine and fellowship, and in breaking of bread, and in prayers."

- Acts 2:44 says, "And all that believed were together, and had all things common."

Point #5: _____

Tithes and offerings are two different types of giving that are a necessary part of living a righteous and obedient life. We know money touches very close to home, but to avoid the topic would be doing a disservice to you and your growing walk with the Lord. According to the Word of God, the first 10 percent of your income belongs to Him. "First" means that when you get paid, you calculate your 10 percent from that, before taxes or anything else. In giving tithes, we recognize that everything already belongs to God, and we are only giving back to Him what He has asked us to give in obedience. It is not just about money; it is about where your heart, faith, and trust are.

Tithes can be used for many things pertaining to the operation of the church, but mainly they provide for the needs of the pastor, church staff, and guest speakers.

➢ Numbers 18:21 says, "And, behold, I have given the children of Levi all the tenth in Israel for an inheritance, for their service which they serve, even the service of the tabernacle of the congregation."

➢ II Chronicles 31:5; Hebrews 7:1–7

Offerings are what you feel in your heart to give or what God impresses upon your heart to give. Offerings can be used to cover the church's regular operating expenses such as utilities, insurance, loan payment, repairs, acts of benevolence, and so on. Sometimes the pastor may ask for a special offering for a project that needs to be done around the church, or maybe a project overseas. Tithes and offerings are not about finances; they are about love, obedience, faith, and devotion. II Corinthians 9:7 says, "Every man according as he purposeth in his heart, so let him give; not grudgingly, or of necessity: for God loveth a cheerful giver." Luke 6:38 says, "Give, and it shall be given unto you; good measure, pressed down, and shaken together, and running over, shall men give into your bosom. For with the same measure that ye mete withal it shall be measured to you again."

Most churches will have envelopes similar to the one below. Envelopes are used to designate where you are intending for that money to go, but this also helps in record-keeping. These records are important for the church (tax records and accountability) and for your personal benefit (tax deductions).

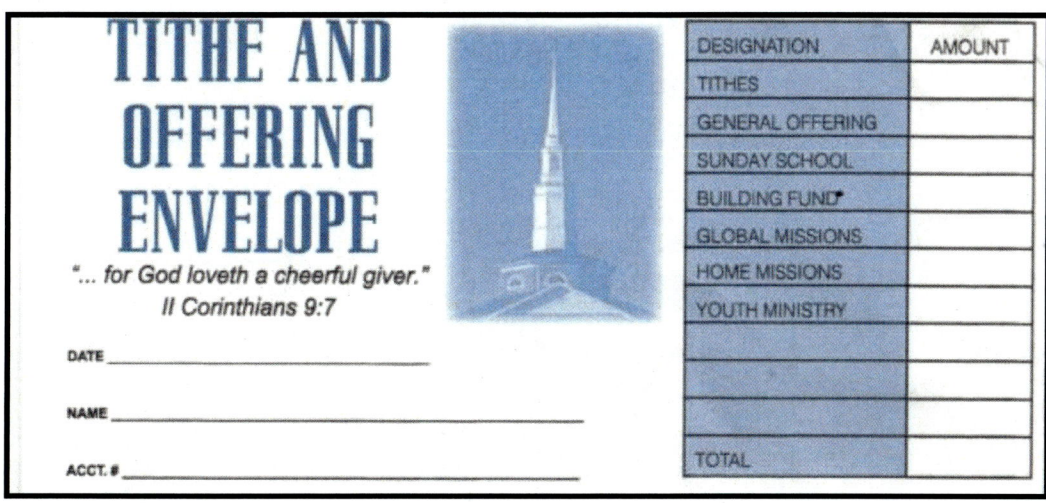

Point #6: We Are His _____

Until Jesus comes back it is our responsibility to "reflect" Him, to be His ambassadors in this world (Mark 16:15; II Corinthians 5:20). In the political world, an ambassador is "an accredited diplomat sent by a country as its official representative to a foreign country." Such a diplomat is expected to look and act appropriately, considering the important business they have with other countries. For example, a French ambassador would not meet the US President wearing jeans and an untucked T-shirt, rolling his eyes and using slang words. Similarly, it is not just about looking and acting the part, but rather being the part—being a true ambassador of Christ. His light should reflect in us through the way we talk (Colossians 4:6), our attitude (Matthew 5:44), and even what we wear (Deuteronomy 22:5). Are we saying the things Jesus would say? Is our demeanor as peaceful and kind as His would be? Would we wear the clothes we are wearing if Jesus asked us to follow Him around and help for a day? Remember the Bible (Word of God) is the final authority. We must be willing to mold ourselves into an image that is pleasing to God. Below are just a few of many scriptural references pertaining to a Christlike lifestyle.

- Colossians 3:17
- Ephesians 4:29
- Colossians 3:8–9, 12–16
- I Corinthians 11
- I Timothy 2:9
- Jeremiah 4:30
- I Peter 3:3–4,
- Leviticus 19:28
- I Peter 1:15–16

Take some time this week and examine yourself (II Corinthians 13:5). Are you trying to create your identity using subculture or peer pressure? Are you identifying with a particular group in an effort to "find yourself"? That is not biblical. You will not find the "self" you are supposed to be while following after what the world offers. As a believer and ambassador, your identity is in Christ. Allow Him to give you personal convictions—both inward and outward—that line up with His Word (Colossians 3:3). Your inward spirituality and outward reflection of that spirituality are of equal importance for _____.

MY NOTES

Week 6 - The Great Commission & Living in Power

Congratulations on being faithful throughout this six-week course. Your life in God is being placed on a firm foundation! In this final session, we will discuss being a witness, sharing our testimony, and how to be a disciple-maker. We will cover the importance of being involved as a member in the body of Christ. We hope by the end of this session you will realize how important you are to people all around you every day, and how much you are needed in your local church body. We pray you will discover ministries you can thrive in and continue to be a blessing to all those around you.

Point #1: A _____ with a _____ to Share: What Is a Witness?

> **Additional Scriptures**
> Proverbs 27:17
> Mark 5:19
> Psalm 66:16
> 1 Peter 4:8-10
> John 14:12
> Luke 10:25-37
> Acts 3:1-10

Witness (Noun): a person who sees an event, typically a crime or accident, take place.
Witness (Verb): have knowledge of (an event or change) from personal observation or experience.

In a courtroom, a witness is someone who describes their personal experience or knowledge of a crime. Witnesses are valued in a courtroom because they have knowledge that other people or even technology may not be able to provide. A firsthand account of an event has more authority and impact than a secondhand account (somebody telling what someone else told them). In the secular world "witnessing" means "watching something happen," but in the church it means "telling what has happened." Just as a witness on the stand tells a jury what they have seen, saints of God can tell other people what they have seen God do.

Each of us is a witness for Jesus because we have personal experiences with Him. We have seen the powerful things He has done and the things He is doing now. Isaiah 43:10 says, "Ye are my witnesses, saith the LORD." Luke 8:39 (ESV) says, "Return to your home, and declare how much God has done for you." Unfortunately, people are not always interested in hearing what God has done for you; they might not even believe in God or believe enough in Him to think He plays any part in the events of a person's life. However, when they see a change in your life or your demeanor, that could spark their curiosity. The change in you could lead them to want to know more about God.

You are a witness; you have a _____. A testimony is a formal written or spoken statement. It is the report the witness gives of the events they saw and experienced. As a part of God's church, your testimony is your report of the ways God has moved in your life. Testimonies are powerful because, even though you may feel alone in your struggles, the reality is that all human beings experience the same types of things, only in slightly different ways. Your story can sound like their story, so the *ending* of your story could give them hope for their own victory. We need to be telling others, both inside and outside the church, about what we have witnessed with Jesus. Revelation 12:11 says, "And they overcame him (the devil) by the blood of the Lamb (Jesus' death on the cross) and by the word of their testimony."

Along with verbally testifying, our lives should be living examples of obeying the plan of salvation (repentance, baptism in the name of Jesus, and receiving the Holy Ghost with the evidence of speaking in tongues). Acts 1:8 says, "But ye shall receive power, after that the Holy Ghost is come upon you: and ye shall be witnesses unto me." We are given power after we receive the Holy Ghost. As God's people, we need to learn to live in that power and authority. *Power* in this verse is derived from the Greek word "dunamis" (pronounced "doo-nah-miss"). This is where we get the word "dynamite." Dynamite is seen and heard! Acts 4:20 says, "For we cannot but speak the things which we have seen and heard."

> **SIDE NOTE:**
>
> When the pastor asks someone to testify, he is asking them to give a report on something specific God has done. That one example could be encouraging to someone. **Your** testimony is your whole story with God; **a** testimony is the report of a specific event.

Point #2: A Disciple of _____ and a Disciple-_____

Matthew 28:19 (NKJV) says, "Go therefore and make disciples of all the nations." This is not a suggestion; it is a *command* to go and make disciples. A disciple is someone who follows a teacher or leader, so making a disciple means being a teacher so a person will have someone to follow. It is important to note that this verse does not say, "Pastors and church leaders, go and make disciples." No, this is a command for *everyone* who lives for God. When you are following Christ, you must encourage others to come behind you. Picture the cars of a train following the engine; the disciples your making are following Christ just as you are, because they are connected to you, and you, in turn, are connected to Christ.

Making a disciple can be a challenge because it is about teaching and leading by example. You will have challenges with your disciples as they struggle to grasp things you may find simple; without being patronizing, you need to have the same patience with a baby in Christ as you would have for a toddler who is learning how to be a "big boy." It is your job to stand by them, encouraging them when they fail and giving advice as they try to learn. Be forgiving and understanding without compromising on what is right.

Finding disciples can be simpler than you might think. Keep your spiritual eyes and ears open for spiritually hungry people (such as coworkers, neighbors, waitresses, etc.). Start out by being their friend. Give them your time by asking them to coffee or listening to their stories. Train yourself to appreciate them sincerely as God does. Everywhere you go, be kind and godly so that people can recognize you as a child of God who has answers, a person to whom they can go for help when they are ready to follow Christ. As you develop a relationship with them, they will ask you questions, and you can teach them what you already know. You will be surprised what God shows you as you begin to follow His Great Commission.

Point #3: Being _____ of the _____ of Christ

I Corinthians 12:14 says, "For the body is not one member, but many." The apostle Paul called us "members of one body" so we can understand the necessity of having different body parts that do different jobs in order for a person to perform a specific task. For example, just opening a door and walking into a room requires eye-hand coordination, balance, and movement of your legs, feet, and arms. Just as diversity is good and necessary in the natural body, diversity is good and necessary in the church. This applies not only to personalities but also to personal giftings or ministries we are involved in.

➤ I Corinthians 12:12 (ESV) says, "For just as the body is one and has many members, and all the members of the body, though many, are one body, so it is with Christ."

➤ I Corinthians 12:17 (ESV) says, "If the whole body were an eye, where would be the sense of hearing? If the whole body were an ear, where would be the sense of smell?"

The Fivefold Ministry: Ephesians 4:11 says "And He gave some, _____; and some, _____; and some, _____; and some, _____ and _____."

➤ Notice that it does not say *some* teachers. We should all be teachers because we should all be making disciples.

Paul goes on to tell us the purpose of the Fivefold Ministry in the church in Ephesians 4:12 "For the perfecting of the saints, for the work of the ministry, for the edifying of the body of Christ."

God also gave us gifts of the Spirit: (I Corinthians 12:7–11): word of wisdom, word of knowledge, faith, healing, miracles, prophecy, discerning of spirits, diverse tongues, interpretation of tongues.

Point #4: Figuring Out What Part of the Body I Am

Where do you see yourself in the future? What fields of ministry or what gifts of the Spirit do you see yourself one day operating in? Though you can ask yourself these questions, it is worth noting that you do not have complete control over this. It is God who provides the gifts or the calling to a specific role. He is the only one perfectly qualified to do this because He knows your past, present, and future experiences along with weaknesses and strengths you may not even know you have. Jesus might call you to things you do not think you want, but that is only because you do not understand yourself or the ministry yet. Because God has a calling for you, He gave you capabilities to operate in that calling and find fulfillment in it. However, submitting to God's authority over your ministry does not mean you are supposed to just sit and wait for God to drop a ministry-specific instruction manual down from the heavens. As you grow in Him, you should seek out what God's will is for you and prepare yourself for ministries you seem to be heading toward. You should explore individual ministries you might eventually be called to, based on your skills, passions, and experiences.

➤ Romans 12:6–8 (ESV) says, "Having gifts that differ according to the grace given to us, let us use them: if prophecy, in proportion to our faith; if service, in our serving; the one that teaches, in his teaching; the one who exhorts [encourage or urge someone], in his exhortation; the one who contributes, in generosity; the one who leads, with zeal [great energy or enthusiasm]; the one who does acts of mercy, with cheerfulness."

Point #5: God's _____ for Your Ministry

A calling is what you do with your life. This requires time and preparation. When God reveals a gift or calling to you, it does not always mean that gift or calling will start immediately. Whenever God reveals His will to you, that means there is something you can do or learn in the present to prepare for greater use in your future. When we discover an earthly job that we want to pursue, we naturally start thinking about the steps it will take to eventually get that job (e.g., going to college, job shadowing, volunteering, etc.) Similarly, when God reveals a ministry He plans to use you for one day, you can start planning ways to prepare for it until it is God's time for you to officially step into that role. We cannot sit idly. Matthew 20:6 says He found "others standing idle and saith unto them, Why stand ye hear all the day idle?" We cannot just wait for that future to arrive. Rather, we must ask ourselves, "What can I do now to help myself grow in the right ways, get experiences that will help in the future, and how can I bless the body now?" That is what Elisha was doing in I Kings 19:19: "So he [Elijah] departed thence and found Elisha, who was plowing with twelve yoke of oxen . . . Elijah passed by him, and cast his mantle upon him." Elisha was working and doing what he could do in the here and now when he received his next calling. Because of Elisha's faithfulness in the waiting, God could trust him with the calling.

When you notice a ministry that the body could be doing but is not, that often is the area God is wanting to use *you* in. Maybe nobody else has done it or will ever think to do it—because it is not their calling to take on. Jesus has revealed this need to *you*. You feel stronger about it than anyone else because it is a burden God has placed on your heart. Instead of waiting for someone else to take on the role you have discovered, instead of questioning why something is not being done, explore how God can use *you* to help meet that need. Take time to talk with your pastor about what the Lord has placed on your heart.

Do not underestimate your power if you are doing what God has called you to do. Be powerful. Fill the void where you are needed. Explore tasks/roles you can take on NOW (or very soon) to prepare for or explore future callings. To help you do this, we have provided a list of ministries on the following page. You may be perfectly qualified for a role you did not even know existed!

Examples of Ministry Opportunities in Your Local Church

Worship/Music Ministry
- Singing on Praise Team/Choir
- Playing an Instrument

Media/Sound Department
- Sound Engineer or Sound Assistant
- Lyric & Announcement Projection

Social Media
- Create Event or Announcement Graphics
- Make posts and monitor church page for engagement and timely responses

Children's Church
- A teacher
- A teacher helper/assistant
- Provide snacks for CC Classes or Events
- Volunteer in Nursery

Youth Department
- Be a Youth Leader
- Volunteer to chaperone and help facilitate Youth Events or Outings
- Provide snacks for Youth Class or Events

Ladies Department
- Help with event planning, decorating

Men's Department
- Help with event planning, decorating

Bible Study Teacher
- Find someone to teach, be a disciple-maker

Prayer Ministry
- Show up to prayer meetings
- Host a prayer meeting or prayer group/book club

Hospitality
- Greeting Guests and Capturing Their Contact Information
- Entering guest information into church's contact system and sending thank you cards for visiting

Bus Ministry
- Being a bus driver or bus driver assistant
- Help facilitate ride list each week

Housekeeping
- Clean the church weekly or on a rotational schedule
- Volunteer to help pick up after events

Groundskeeper
- Mowing the lawn
- Snow removal via plowing or shoveling
- Gardening
- Picking up trash on the exterior of church

Jail/Prison Ministry

Church Secretary

Treasurer/Accountant

MY NOTES

Made in the USA
Monee, IL
23 December 2024